MEXICO
and
CENTRAL AMERICA

Troll Associates

MEXICO
and
CENTRAL
AMERICA

by Keith Brandt

Illustrated by Allan Eitzen

Troll Associates

Library of Congress Cataloging in Publication Data

Brandt, Keith, (date)
    Mexico and Central America.

    Summary: A brief description and history of Mexico
and Central America.
        1. Mexico—Juvenile literature.   2. Central America—
Juvenile literature.   [1. Mexico.   2. Central America]
I. Eitzen, Allan, ill.   II. Title.
F1208.5.B73   1985   972   84-2668
ISBN 0-8167-0264-0 (lib. bdg.)
ISBN 0-8167-0265-9 (pbk.)

Hundreds of years ago, before the first
European explorers arrived, there were great
empires in Mexico and Central America.
Today only their names—the Olmec and
Toltec, Zapotec and Maya and Aztec—
remain, along with the weathered stone
ruins of their temples and statues.

Gone are the customs and religions the
people of these empires followed. Gone,
too, are the cultures and cities that flour-
ished long ago.

Now in the lands of the great Indian empires are eight modern nations in which the past and the present are tightly woven together. This is true of the people, too. Most of the population of Mexico and the seven Central American countries are mestizos. A mestizo is a person who has both Indian and European ancestors.

The main language spoken in all these countries is Spanish, which was brought by the explorers from Spain. But mixed in with this Latin American Spanish are many Indian words. And there are still small villages where some of the old Indian languages are spoken.

In Mexico and Central America, the old and new are blended in many ways. There are large cities with skyscrapers, television studios, movie theaters, and modern conveniences. And there are poor farms without electricity and plumbing, where crops of corn and vegetables are planted and harvested by hand, just as they were before the invention of farm machinery.

There are large universities and fine hospitals and museums. But many people cannot read or write and have never seen a doctor.

There are restaurants where the finest international foods are served. But many people still grind their own corn and bake the corn cakes called tortillas in outdoor clay ovens, just as their Indian ancestors did so long ago.

There are people dressed in blue jeans and running shoes or business suits or any of the latest fashions. But others wear thong sandals or go barefoot and dress in loose cotton garments, colorful shawls, and beads, as did their Indian ancestors.

The lands of Mexico and Central America, rich in the heritage of the past, lie between the North American country of the United States and the South American country of Colombia. Along their eastern shore are the warm waters of the Gulf of Mexico and the Caribbean Sea. And to the west of Mexico and Central America is the Pacific Ocean.

North America

United States

Mexico

Central America

Colombia

South America

Mountains

Central Plateau

Mountains

Mexico is far larger than all the countries of Central America combined. Two mountain chains run down through the country, from the northwest to the southeast. The land between these mountain ranges is the high Central Plateau of Mexico, where most of the people live.

The northern half of the plateau is flat and receives little rainfall. Further south is the Bajió. Here, there is enough rain to grow crops of cereal grains, such as wheat and barley. The southern edge of the central plateau is a rugged mountain range with rich volcanic soil and active volcanoes.

The Gulf Coast of Mexico is dry toward the north. But further south, there are tropical rain forests and fertile farm lands.

The Pacific Coast has steep mountain slopes in the south and rich farm lands in the north.

To the northwest—almost completely separated from the rest of Mexico—is a long peninsula known as Lower California. The climate here is dry, and much of the land is desert.

The southeast part of Mexico is the Yucatán Peninsula, which separates the Gulf of Mexico from the Caribbean Sea. It is a limestone plateau with dry bushlands in the north and tropical rain forests in the south.

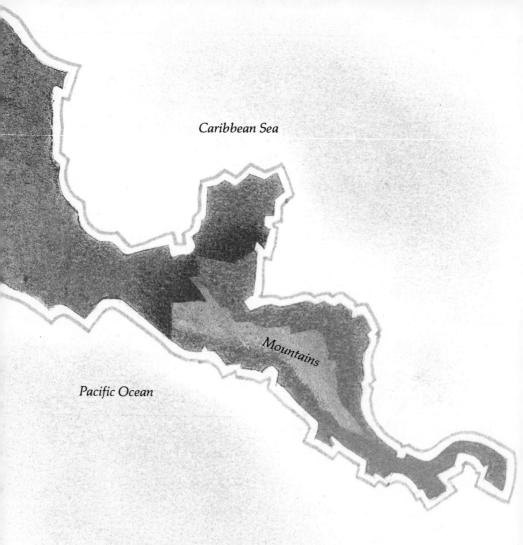

Caribbean Sea

Mountains

Pacific Ocean

In Central America, the land along the shores of the Caribbean Sea is a coastal plain with jungles and swamps. On the Pacific coast is a narrow plain that receives less rainfall. And running down through much of Central America is a highland region with several volcanic mountains.

18

Central America is made up of the colony of Belize, which was formerly called British Honduras, and the republics of Guatemala, Honduras, El Salvador, Nicaragua, Costa Rica, and Panama. Panama is cut by the Panama Canal, which joins the Caribbean Sea with the Pacific Ocean.

The history of Central America and Mexico begins as early as 10,000 B.C., when Indians came down from the north. They were hunters, but by 5000 B.C., they had begun to grow corn, beans, squash, and other crops.

As they settled down to farm, they established small villages. The villages slowly expanded and grew larger, and civilization spread to the coasts and south into what is now Guatemala.

Between A.D. 300 and A.D. 900, there were advanced civilizations in central and southern Mexico, in the Yucatán Peninsula, and in Central America. The Maya Indians built pyramids and temples. The Zapotec Indians built temples, tombs, and plazas in a mountaintop city in southern Mexico.

Then, during the 900s, the Toltec Indians became the dominant tribe. Their empire centered north of what is now Mexico City and reached as far as the Yucatán Peninsula.

The final great Indian empire was built by the Aztecs. When they first reached Mexico's Central Valley, about eight hundred years ago, the Aztecs were a primitive, warlike, nomadic tribe. They were used to staying in one place for a year or so, taking everything they could from the land and the people, then moving on. Because of their cruelty and warlike nature, the Aztecs were feared and hated everywhere they went.

The wandering of the Aztecs came to an end when they reached the fertile Central Valley. They conquered all the other tribes in the region and began a rule that lasted hundreds of years. In the Aztec capital of Tenochtitlán, near present-day Mexico City, they built fine palaces, beautiful gardens, large temples, and statues of frightening gods.

The city also had bridges, canals, and aqueducts, as well as schools and large public squares. In the squares were great open markets where merchants sold jewels, clothing, food, knives and swords, pottery, herbs, animal hides, and many other items. The Aztec civilization was very rich and productive. But it was also terrifying, because the Aztecs believed in offering human sacrifices.

The Aztec empire thrived until the Spanish, under Hernando Cortés, arrived in 1519. Then, in just two years, Cortés conquered the Aztecs and their mighty emperor, Montezuma. The capital city was reduced to rubble. Cortés, with an army of only 560 men and a number of Indians, had brought down the powerful Aztec empire.

Cortés was able to do this partly because of an Indian myth. When the Spanish captain landed on the east coast of Mexico, the Aztecs were certain that he was Quetzalcoatl —the Feathered Serpent.

The Feathered Serpent was an ancient god who had brought knowledge and skills to the Indians, then walked east, into the sea, and disappeared— after promising to return one day. So the Aztecs were not prepared to fight, but to welcome this visitor from the east.

The Spanish language and the Catholic religion, brought by Cortés and his countrymen, are still dominant in Mexico and Central America. But the old Spanish system of huge estates owned by one person and worked by many landless peasants has at last begun to change.

Nevertheless, most of the people in the Central American countries are still very poor and do not own land. They work on huge banana and coffee plantations in Guatemala, El Salvador, Honduras, Nicaragua, Costa Rica, and Panama. In addition, they mine and market zinc, nickel, copper, gold, and silver. They also work in factories, producing manufactured goods.

Mexico is much richer than any of the Central American countries. It is the world's leading producer of silver, and among the leaders in the production of sulfur, lead, and zinc. In addition, Mexico has a vast supply of oil and natural gas.

Mexican industry turns out cars, textiles, steel, heavy machinery, and just about anything that any major industrial nation produces. This industry and the country's natural resources are helping to improve Mexico's economic condition.

The history of Mexico and Central America has been marked by centuries of war, poverty, and struggle. Yet today, medicine, education, and technology are making advances and helping to improve the standard of living in much of Mexico and Central America.